# yellow

# yellow

Mrs. Davis' Class
Make someone's day yellow!
2019

adam peterson

yellow



ISBN-13: 978-1497319776
ISBN-10: 1497319773

Text Set In Adobe Noteworthy

for my friend, Honor

This is **NOT** a story about the color yellow.

This is not a story about COLORS at all.

In fact, this is a story about a person.

It's a story about a person
who was a friend to everyone she met.
Some people said she was "everyone's friend."

This is a story about my friend, Honor.

This is my friend, Honor! She was the kind of friend who made others happy just by being herself!

She saw the good in everyone and every situation, even when everyone else could only see the bad.

I’m sure she felt bad sometimes, but she was too busy making other people happy to get sad too often!

She turned people's gray skies into...

...YELLOW

skies!

Honor brightened A LOT of skies
because she had a A LOT of friends!
She was a kindergarten teacher.
She was the teacher who
everyone wanted to get!

People loved how nice and cheerful she was.
Everyone loved the way she sang
funny songs and danced to the music
from her old record player!

Her classroom was very bright
and welcoming too!
It was the yellow room!

A B C D

Like most girls I know, Honor loved shoes!
She had A LOT of shoes!

She wore warm, furry boots when it was cold.

She wore fancy tennis shoes to run fast!

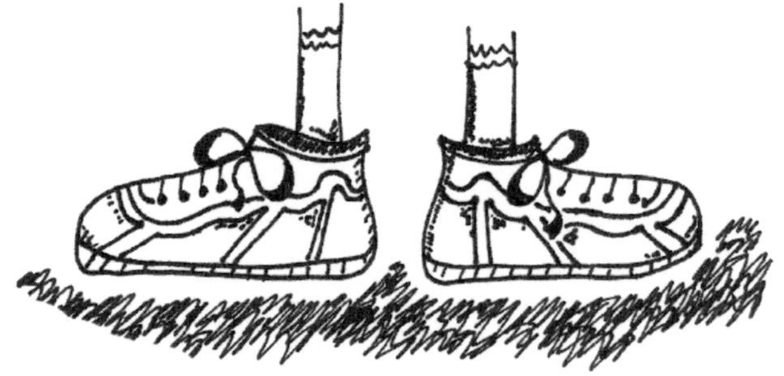

The best shoes she ever wore were
her bright yellow shoes!

When she wore these, people would say,
"Nice shoes, Honor!"

I think she liked that.

Honor wasn't just a friend to people.
She loved animals too,
especially horses!

She loved to ride horses and even taught me how to ride one!

Well, she almost taught me how.

She loved to take care of her old, gray horse named Rusty!

She loved to ride her
tall, brown horse named Vinnie!

I bet if she could have found one,
Honor would have bought a yellow horse too!

Do you have a friend with a very unique laugh?
I did, and it was Honor!

Her laugh was so unique that it's hard to describe.

It sort of sounded like a little, yellow bird chirping loudly as it attempted its first flight...

...well, kind of.

Honor would laugh and then...

...babies would laugh...

...kids would laugh...

...and even grown-ups would laugh!

I have many memories of Honor
that I hope I never forget.

But I do have one I wish I could forget.

I wish I could forget the phone call I got
when Honor got sick.

She was sick with the kind of sick
that doctors can't fix. Her doctor told her
she had cancer and gave her bad news.
I'm sure she cried when her doctor left,
but when I went to see her, she was smiling.
She didn't want any of her friends
to feel sad for her, so she found a way
to keep herself happy! No matter how
sick or weak she got, one thing never changed.

Honor never stopped smiling!

Everyone has a friend like Honor, right?
Think about it for a moment.
Who is your friend who always makes you laugh?
Who is your friend who always sees the good in you?
Who is your friend that smiles no matter what?
Find that person, sit them down, and thank them
for making your life and the lives of others more...

...YELLOW!

The REAL Honor:

The character in this story is based on my real friend, Honor. Honor was a kindergarten teacher and loved to listen to records in her classroom! She adored her horses and loved sharing this hobby with others. She really did have the most contagious and unique laugh I have ever heard. It didn't, however, sound like a small bird. To this day, no words come to mind to accurately describe Honor's laugh. Honor was a wife and a mother, and her family meant the world to her. She really was "everyone's friend", and she could always find the good in any situation no matter how bad it was. Honor did get sick and was diagnosed with cancer at the young age of 59. She lost her courageous battle against this ugly disease three days shy of her 60th birthday. Honor was loved by many and is remembered by all the people who were lucky enough to know her.

Oh, and she really did love the color yellow.

## About The Author

Adam Peterson is a husband, father, and kindergarten teacher. When he isn't writing, he enjoys biking, playing guitar, and playing outside with his kids!  He lives in Illinois with his wife and two children.

Made in the USA
Lexington, KY
29 May 2019